Changes by the Ticking of the Clock
'A Collection of Poetry'

Hannah Louise Thornton

Changes by the Ticking of the Clock
'A Collection of Poetry'

Copyright © by Hannah Louise Thornton 2014

Published by Lulu Publishing Company

www.lulu.com

All rights reserved. Without limiting the rights under copyright reserved above, no part of this publication may be stored in, reproduced, or introduced into a retrieval system, or transmitted, in any form, or by any means (electronic, photocopying, recording, mechanical, or otherwise) without the prior written permission from the copyright owner of this book.

ISBN: 978 - 1 – 291 – 73609 – 0

Dedication of book - 5
Dear Mum – 6
Dad – 8
Can Death be Called Fair? - 10
Life is a Blossoming Rose – 11
Farewell - 15
Man on a Ledge – 17
The Life We Live – 18
Family – 19
The Game – 21
The Weather – 23
The Doll – 25
I'm Sorry - 27
Through the Fog – 28
Remember the Journey – 29
Goodbye, Sweet Angel – 30
The Eyes of the Child – 32
Never Ending Cycle – 35
You All Know *That* Person - 37
The Tattoo – 39
The Choice – 41
The Broken Heart – 42
The Ice Will Always Break – 44
Catch My Breath – 46
The World behind the Door – 48
I am Always There – 50
A Precious Treasure – 54
Dark Changes – 56

The Ticking of the Clock - 58
Moulding Minds – 60
Love Poem without the Letter 'e' - 62
So Many Names – 63
My Words Part Us – 65
My Eyes – 67
My Final Words – 69

Dedication

I dedicate this book to my mum for always standing by me through the thick and thin and never giving up on my dreams even when other people did or when they told me I could never make it.

I've thought for years of how to thank you and this is the only way I can.

Forever and always my love to my mum.

Dear Mum

You are my best friend and I will love you always and forever.

Dear mum,
For nine months I was in your tum,
And for eighteen years,
You've chased away my fears.

When I was crying,
And claimed I was dying,
You made it all right,
I was never alone in the fight.

Now that I'm older,
Things sometimes feel colder,
But now it's my turn,
I'm ready to learn.

Never feel alone,
I'm always at the end of the phone,
If you ever need me,
I'll be there, you'll see.

I'll fight your fights,
And help you reach new heights,
I'll stand by you,
In everything you do.

I'll forever be there,
Because I will always care,
I'll make you proud,
I've even vowed.

I am your daughter,
I'll make the slaughter,
To keep you harmless,
I'd go armless.

No risk is too great,
Against those you hate,
I'll run the distance,
To be your armed resistance.

My words can be cruel,
It'll make 'em all drool,
I'll wipe away your tears,
And I'll battle your fears.

Because no matter what,
You've given me a lot,
Now I'll give some,
You're my amazing mum.

Dad

To my dad, I will love you forever no matter what.

You stand proud and tall,
Forever there to protect us,
You fight back the icy winds,
The hail, the rain and the snow,
Never have you left me alone,
Throughout it all you've remained.

Until now I didn't realise
How much you truly did for me,
I ask your forgiveness and love,
Although I do not always deserve it,
I know you will never stop,
I hate how long this has taken.

When I cried, you held me,
When I needed your help, you gave it,
Even when I pushed you away,
You caught me when I fell,
We laugh, and joke, and fight and cry,
But our love is forever.

Sometimes you embarrass me,
Your dancing, wow, that's scary,
But no matter how much I may blush and hide,
I am proud to call you my dad,

The blushing and hiding ends today,
For I realise now the pain it causes.

We joke and say, if I make it one day,
You say you will embarrass me,
And I say go for it,
I will not deny being your daughter,
I will encourage and join you,
Because I am the younger you.

I love the fun and laughs we have,
I hate the times we fight and glare,
I want our fun to be forever,
No matter what, I promise to never change,
No money, or fame, or power or time
Will ever change who I am.

I am proud to call you dad,
I hope you feel the same about me,
You say your job is not special and important,
You say you did nothing with your life,
But I couldn't be happier than I am now,
Boring job or not, your job as my dad was perfect.

Can Death be Called Fair?

Can death be called fair when a babe is born still?
Can death be called fair when an infant is taken ill?
Can death be called fair when the good die so young?
Can death be called fair when the night robbers run?

Can death be called fair when a hero dies alone?
Can death be called fair when too far to reach is the phone?
Can death be called fair when a parent buries their child?
Can death be called fair when no one is found but the name is still filed?

At the end of the day, death is not fair,
For the good die young, while the bad live on with so little as a care,
Why he does this, we do not know,
But death has never been lower than the lowest of the low.

Life is a Blossoming Rose

Life is like a rose they say,
Blossoms in the day,
But withers in the night,
And without that bit of light,
Life will shrivel and die.

A baby's breath is white they say,
Pure and innocent night and day,
We all protect the babes we love,
Similar to the sacred dove,
A baby's breath will save us all.

A toddler is a sweet monster they say,
Smiley and bubbly during the day,
But make the mistake of getting it riled,
And you will soon have a demon child,
A toddler is a moulding tool.

A child is a gift from God they say,
Ever present during the day,
Late at night the parents breathe,
For no matter what they cannot leave,
A child is a trophy, an honour, a gift.

A teenager is a sulker they say,
Moods and attitude across the day,

Do not worry it is just a faze,
Open your eyes and it will be but a haze,
The path of a teenager has just begun.

By the time you reach twenty you know it all they say,
Thinking you know the world by day,
But still messing up by the light of the night,
Your fall from your godlike status is not such a great height,
At twenty you are still a learning child.

At thirty you will have a meltdown they say,
How embarrassing in the light of day,
You have so many years of wonder to live,
Never say no because you have more to give,
Do not be dull, you are thirty and proud.

Society is a façade they say,
Playing nicely with others throughout the day,
Only to turn beneath the moon,
Perhaps it is not those that are the loon,
Society is a bitter sweet asylum.

By forty, by god you've done it they say,
Looking your best through the day,
By this time you have realised society is wrong,
And you were a fool to play for so long,
You have finally realised at the age of forty.

At fifty you're sick of it all they say,
Tired of all the lies in a day,
Planning ahead the next twenty years,
Brushing away all of your fears,
Retirement is soon and you're ready for it.

At sixty you're articulate they say,
I can't always agree when I listen to the day,
Most often a grumpy old cod,
You're certain you're gonna be under the sod,
Sixty is a bitter age.

Seventy wow, I hope I get there they say,
Starting to fall asleep in the day,
Still smiling at guests,
For no one is any longer a pest,
At seventy you're weakening slowly.

By eighty you truly do know it all they say,
Many an hour you sleep in the day,
Look at the fantastic waves of silver hair,
Wow, they look so regal in their comfy old chair,
By eighty you're a teacher, an onlooker and a listener.

The grim reaper comes for all they say,
He does not care if he is seen in the day,
Nor does he take only the wicked and bad,
But no matter who I suppose it's sad,

For the reaper does not care.

Everybody dies they say,
Whether in the dark of night or the light of day,
In pain or at peace,
Each of our heartbeats will eventually cease,
Because everybody lives and dies.

Farewell

As the skies release the rain,
Sets in that everlasting pain,
We lay you slowly down to rest,
I feel in my heart that I failed the test.

My heart, how it bleeds,
As the priest reads,
I was not there,
Despite how much I care.

My love lives on,
Though I know I will receive none,
There is a cruel burn,
Why was I too late to learn?

It will never happen to us we said,
But now you lay there still and dead,
Why did you not say?
Now there will never be a day.

We will never meet,
Remember our feet,
How they marked the sand,
And how you offered your hand.

God bless you sweet child,
So often your number I dialled,
Goodbye to your soft grace,
I will forever remember your smiling face.

Man on a Ledge

A world on the edge,
A man on a ledge,
No difference in size,
Despite the vicious lies

How can we judge?
We sit here and nudge,
What do we know,
About someone who's low?

We move in the rush,
We brush off and hush,
What we don't like,
We send on a hike,

We all close our eyes,
And cry when the problem dies,
Listen and stop,
Before that final drop,

Just give a little time,
It doesn't cost a dime,
The world isn't on the edge,
But there is always someone on a ledge.

The Life We Live

Bitter sweet is the life we live,
When all we do is give,
Without so much as a thank you,
What is it we truly live to do?

Family

No matter how embarrassing and annoying we may all be, I'll never stop loving each and every one of you.

A family is bitter sweet,
We live and love and fight and cuss,
But the moment one of us suffers,
We all jump to make a fuss.

You drive me up the wall,
But after all at the end of the day,
We all love each other,
No matter what we may say.

We are many different people,
And yet all the same,
We don't always see in time,
And we lose each other, what a shame.

Forever together,
Bound by blood,
I will never stop fighting,
Although I did all I could.

You embarrass me so,
But I stand strong and proud,
I will never deny you,

Despite the disapproving crowd.

You cannot chose your family,
But I chose you,
Forever my family,
I will forever be true.

We stand together,
Through thick and thin,
No matter what you do,
We will forgive your sin.

My love will live on,
Even after the day I die,
I will protect and love you,
And that is no lie.

The Game

Some believe love is a serious thing,
They tell you love is vital,
Important in everyone's life,
And yet there are so many that play love like a game.

A game to cause pain,
A game to play with their friends,
A game to play simply to steal what comes next,
A vicious game that scars even the toughest players.

However, there are some that play nicely,
They play to find love,
They play to be happy,
They play to make others feel the same.

In every game you will find cheaters,
In every game you will find happiness,
In every game there will be a loser,
Not all games are as brutal as this.

A game can be fun,
A game can be boring,
A game can be long and hard,
A game can be short and sweet.

Everyone wants to play this game,
But why this one?
Why the game that causes so much pain,
Is it not better to be happy alone?

Love your friends and family,
Why would they hurt you?
Love a stranger and face whatever they throw,
You have everything to lose, but so do they.

Love because you live,
Love because you can,
Love because it's what you want,
Love because it makes you happy.

Never settle for anything less,
Make sure you strive for only the best,
Not everyone is out to play,
But make sure they're right for you to stay.

The Weather

How I love the rain,
Although many call it mundane,
To jump in the puddles,
And it brings about warm cuddles.

The sun is so bright,
It offers warm light,
We hate the burn,
Yet we refuse to learn.

Ah that pretty white snow,
I believe some call it their foe,
So soft it falls like a feather,
And yet it can be as tough as leather.

The wind does swirl,
And makes pretty girls twirl,
It cracks fast like a whip,
And bites with a nip.

All hail to the king,
What a painful thing,
We fight off the pain,
Oh how it drives me insane.

We always moan,
There goes the ever present drone,
We close our eyes to what should be seen,
And we complain about the simple because we're not keen.

The weather is here,
Stop exaggerating your fear,
Some people have it worse than you,
So smile and be thankful that you're not there too.

How I laugh at your whining,
Just look for the silver lining,
Breathe deep and exhale,
It is not a contest, you will not fail.

So your hair is a mess,
No one could care less,
Oh well what a shame,
But everyone looks the same.

The Doll

An angel,
A doll,
A possession,
A prize.

A seductress,
A witch,
A devil,
A bitch.

You're innocent,
You're strong,
You're dangerous,
You're a lady.

You're an ornament to be shown,
A silent beauty never allowed to moan,
You accepted your place,
The smile never left your delicate face.

But now here I stand,
I offer my hand,
You are forever free,
I give you my life, you see.

Too long silent and weak,
It's your turn to speak,
You're free to go,
No more lying low.

Run and I will break the chains,
I will never release the reigns,
I am the extreme,
Your freedom is my dream.

No one suspect beauty behind the tattoos,
They all point and stare and laugh and accuse,
How simple your mind,
You are completely blind.

You want me loyal,
But instead I coil,
I will bring you down,
I am unfazed by your frown.

Your power is gone,
I am forever yours to call on,
But now I can stand alone,
Free to be on my own.

I'm Sorry

I'm sorry for the times I wasn't there,
I know you needed me, it wasn't fair,
When I look back, I know it's true,
I was selfish and never there for you.

I'm sorry that it took so long to see,
It wasn't you, it was always me,
And now I regret it all,
I never should have let you fall.

And now I say I'm sorry again,
Behind your smile, I see your pain,
I never deserved someone special like you,
We used to be stuck together like glue.

I'm sorry, oh why did I let you go,
My love, I have never been lower than low,
And yet here I kneel, before you at last,
Desperate to regain our lost but never forgotten past.

Through the Fog

The night was cold,
Only a hand to hold,
The fog was thickening,
And the smell almost sickening.

The lights they flickered,
While drunken sailors snickered,
The waves gently swayed,
The ships appear and fade.

Three times it swung,
The thick fog hung,
And then it rose,
To reveal my foes.

The pirates they're here,
They smirk and they sneer,
I turn to escape this hoard,
But freeze at the stab of that cold sword.

How could I fall for their tricks?
I lay here dying while they get their kicks,
I sink deep beneath the crushing water,
While they return to their vicious slaughter.

Remember the Journey
'Lest We Forget'

Silence falls on the twilight hour,
Across the field there stands a flower,
How beautiful it looks when not bound,
And beneath there lays the never found.

A willow protects the fallen as it weeps,
Weeping for all the secrets it always keeps,
How and when the blossom fell,
Came similar to the heroes forced into hell.

It was not the battle but the body that died,
It was the brave that fought while the weak did hide,
With no care, only a flick of the wrist,
The weak compiled that dreaded list.

Oh how they leapt and jumped over barbed wire,
Throwing themselves into enemy fire,
Happiness returned after the lifting of their souls,
But forever in our hearts remain cold holes.

Goodbye, Sweet Angel

We hear so oft' on the news,
A sweet child taken from the world,
We hate to hear those vicious words,
But we refuse to see what is before us,
A bruise, a sob, a silence.

We lose innocence so quickly in life,
The world cannot afford to lose any more,
The Lord Almighty protects his angels,
We are all his children,
Why does he let pain exist?

We each have an angel and a demon beside us,
We must choose between the two,
Make your choice the angel,
Do not stray from the light of God,
For all that waits is Hell.

Stray from god and fall from grace,
All you will cause is pain and suffering,
The demon makes you do cruel things,
Steal, kidnap, murder and rape,
Be strong and fight him back.

Oh that sweet, sweet angel,
So weak and frail,
Unable to fight back the demon you hold,
Not even their angel can help the child,
For you are strong and brutal and wild.

But now you stand and weep and sob,
You claim you do not remember a thing,
How dare you claim to love that child?
When it is you that stole them from the world,
You that ruined and broke the child.

How vicious a monster you even lie!
'I didn't do it, I love my child',
But you lie no more,
For the evidence is clear,
You will rot in a cell and then burn in Hell.

No punishment is great enough
For the crimes you commit,
You were not fit to have that sweet child,
Wipe away your tears, you have no right,
Now we say goodbye to that beautiful, sweet, sweet angel.

The Eyes of the Child

Mummy wakes me up at seven,
I heard one day she'll go to heaven,
I don't want mummy to live with God,
She's not his; she's mine, mhmm, and nod.

Mummy smiles and gives me a hug,
Ooh what's that? A really big bug,
I'll follow it and see,
Ouch mummy, I hurt my knee!

'Time to get ready for school' she says,
I don't like going, they're really long days,
'You only go for three stupid hours',
My brother says I'm silly like the Lego towers.

Ooh look a red racing car,
When you push it, it doesn't go far,
Let me wash it in my milk and see what you do,
'Darling don't do that, the car is brand new'.

Daddy looks funny with that silly old tie,
Mummy says he's stressed so I have to lie,
My brother said that daddy was fired,
I don't know what that means, mummy, I'm tired.

'Whatcha eating there, buddy?'
'Go upstairs and take off that hoodie',
Mummy shouts but daddy just smiles,
'Darling, she never talks to me. Have you seen my files?'

Bye, bye daddy, I'm going to school,
He kisses me quickly and calls my brother a tool,
I want to sit in the front now, mummy,
Not until you're old enough to not have a dummy.

Look mummy, up there, there's a big bird,
'I bet she's gonna be a total nerd',
'Be nice to your sister or you'll have to walk',
Mummy starts the game of nobody talk.

Mummy smiles and says 'we're here',
My brother laughs and waves and says 'goodbye *dear*',
Oh mummy, look! Toys. Can we play hide and seek?
'Not today sweetie, a plumber is coming about the leak'.

Where's mummy? I want to go home,
'Why don't you come and play with this foam',
Ooh look, it's all white,
'Wow, it's so light'.

It's the end of the day,
Oh look, mummy has come to play,
'What is that all over your dress?'

Look what I made, it's called cress.

Mummy says 'I think it's time you had a nap',
I don't want one, but I'll sit on your lap,
Mummy smiles and starts to count sheep,
It's not long before I'm fast asleep.

Never Ending Cycle

You claim you're so perfect,
Yet we all know you're not,
If you lie and you cheat,
Your relationship will rot.

You call her your bitch,
You lie to her face,
But if in return
I bet you would not continue the chase.

Stop all these lies,
You've got a good girl,
Is losing her really worth
Watching a pretty girl twirl?

Thanks to your actions,
Your girl is now broken,
Too hurt to ever see,
That she can offer her sweet token.

And so now she is bitter,
Twisted and cold,
Her heart is pure ice,
And will remain when she's old.

But now you feel guilty,
You beg her to come back,
And if she should fall,
We say it is the brain that she lacks.

To punish you know,
She repeats your own act,
This is a never ending cycle,
And that is a fact.

You All Know *That* Person

Alright, come and sit down,
You've tarnished your crown,
You're so full of crap,
I can even write a rap.

You're living in a dream,
That's breaking at the seam,
With your stupid *not* dyed hair,
Crawl back to your lair.

You're gonna get a slap,
And you're gonna need a cap,
Say hi to the fat lip,
Welcome to your sinking ship.

I don't know why you were hired,
Surely you're gonna get fired,
You mess everything up,
Sorry I'm a half empty cup.

You just don't get it,
That dim bulb ain't lit,
Get off your phone,
I'm sick of your drone.

Do your damn job,

You make me wanna sob,
We can all see,
So don't push me.

You're ignorant and rude,
Your jokes are just crude,
Your music sucks,
You care too much about your looks.

Just stop the lying,
We're all crying,
You're such a joke,
Call yourself a bloke?

You're a total chicken,
You need a good kickin',
Why don't you see?
One and one don't make three.

I hope your baby makes you,
'Cause you act like you're two,
What does she see?
Because you ain't never shown me.

You could be cool,
But instead you're a tool,
If you give it out you take it back,
Now there's something else you lack.

The Tattoo

I know you think it's stupid,
And I know you think I don't care,
I know you think I'm reckless,
And I know you hate it there.

People will always judge me,
People will always stop and stare,
People will be forever cruel,
And people will never be fair.

So they say I'm rough and hard,
They watch me as I walk,
Their watching eyes don't bother me,
And sometimes I smile as I listen to them talk.

What they will never understand
Is that it was never made for them,
My tattoo is here and mine to show,
And I am proud to raise my hem.

Although my morals, you deem old fashioned,
My creativity shines on through,
My body is a blank canvas,
The tattoos redesign and make me new.

The world is changing every day,

And although you fear for my career,
Now that I bare the mark of ink,
I am proud to say my mind is clear.

Today I stand, filled with confidence,
Because of the beauty of my tattoo,
I smile and laugh and talk and shrug,
For their words can never make me blue.

I already have faced rejection and hate,
But now I look back with a proud smile,
I made it this far in my life,
And I did it my own way, in my style.

The Choice

We each stand upon the line,
With the same decision to make,
Do we fall right or left, back and forth?
Whichever you chose, you will be judged,
Whether it be in the grace of God or by the hounds of Hell,
We will all fall or rise.

From the moment we arrive on this Earth,
Until the very second we die,
The celestial and sinister battle for your soul,
Who will win, you will decide,
You will rise or fall through the choices you make,
The choice is yours, make it right.

The Broken Heart

It was early winter
The day you never showed,
I should have listened to my head,
And stayed at home in the warm,
But instead, I followed my heart,
Only to find the cold rejection
That I already knew awaited me.

For a time
My heart was broken,
But I soon saw the light,
I was always better off without you,
It's a shame I wasted so much time
On someone who never cared,
But now I know the mistake I made, it will not happen twice.

People said I was better than you,
But I was blinded by your lies,
Weak and foolish, like a child.
Despite the bitter cold I felt,
I hope it never happens to you,
But then, I doubt it will,
Forever the one to cause the pain.

Now I look back, I ask myself,
Was it really my heart that was broken?

The truth is, you never touched it,
Perhaps you hurt nothing but my pride,
I know now, you were not worth the tears,
But at the time, I felt the need to cry,
While now I laugh and smile at you.

And so, I suppose now
I owe you a thank you,
You taught me who not to follow,
Now I will not fall so fast and hard,
I will never be made a fool of again,
And so, my dear, I thank you,
For never touching my heart.

The Ice Will Always Break

Once again I am the fool,
In your never ending parade of lies,
The argument soon dies to silence,
And the bitterness of your words scars me
While the memories remain upon my heart.
To shield me from the striking pain,
The ice returns to trap my breaking heart,
Not even your words of love can crack through,
But here we wear the smiles of old.
Beneath the sun we hide the pain,
Our lies are well hidden in the bright
Burning light they worship.
The war inside me rages on,
With every sweet compliment and gesture,
I feel the ice thickening,
The chill has almost reached my brain,
Not long now before it's all over,
Why should I live on in doubt?
Your words did scar my body and soul,
I know you cannot take them back,
But I heard that they were in you,
How can we return to the life we had?

But now, you stand before me,
The salty tears of sorrow for what you have lost,
My heart is frozen,

What is it you intend to do now?
Your tears mean nothing to me,
I care not for your pain after your bitter words.
The chances are gone,
The story is repeating in my mind,
The secrets unravelling and swirling inside me,
But no tears fall from my eyes,
My ice has spread to my eyes and glazed them.
But what is this?
You confess your sins so freely to me,
Why do you tell me your secrets?
I feel the ice melt in my eyes and the tears fall,
The ice is melting and I have not allowed it,
I wipe away the tears and turn away,
The ice will never melt.
As you talk, the pain strikes hard,
I gasp and hold my chest,
The ice is breaking from my heart.
The hatred fades away and you were honest with me.
Melted and forgiven after the breaking of the ice.

Catch My Breath

My breath catches at the sight of your lips,
My memory did you no justice,
I see you so oft' in my dreams
And imagine the perfection of your kiss.
But now I stand here,
My words lost in the oblivion of love
As I wait in the rain,
Allowing the cool water to wash away my imperfections.
Your eyes glisten in the light of the porch,
Your dress dances in the breeze to some unknown song,
And your hair,
Oh, your hair drapes and sways so beautifully.

Here, before you, I feel safe,
Safe in the knowledge that you are watching only me,
The sound of your smile moves me,
Yes. Your smile has a sound.
I barely know you and yet I know everything,
You laugh at the rain and pull me beneath the porch,
The world around me blurs as your arms hold me.
No words exchanged,
I feel the world fall far beneath,
We are almost flying without the wings of angels,
Nothing can part us now,
Except perhaps that.

The door of your house opens,
Your father bursts out,
But you do not release me,
Nor do you break the sweetness of our kiss.
I feel his eyes burning into my skull,
When we break, I turn and watch him,
But you laugh the gentlest of laughs
And warn him off.
He moves to leave but stops and glares,
I move my hand quickly up your back,
But it is too late,
He already saw my fingers trace your lower back.

You move to block him,
But he pushes you aside
So I turn and run, the laughter growing inside me,
Or is it hysteria?
I have no breath, how can I run so fast?
I glance back through the rain and smile,
You stand by the door,
Your eyes glisten in the light of the porch,
Your dress dances in the breeze to some unknown song,
And your hair,
Oh your hair drapes and sways so beautifully.
And then you are gone until I hold you again.

The World behind the Door

We do not believe what we cannot see,
We turn away from the signs,
Block out the sounds,
And shy away from the truth
When we are needed the most.

It is not always clear, and so
We are not always to blame,
But if the signs are there,
Why do we not see them?
Do we turn away out of cruelty or fear?

If that is the case,
Why do they do nothing?
They say fear is a great motivator,
And yet nothing changes
When the fear is there.

They need us to be strong,
They need us to stand up and protect them,
To be there when they are ready to talk,
To listen and comfort when they need a kind word,
We must be there to make them strong.

No one in this world is alone,
There is always someone there to listen,

Whether we know they are there or not,
Someone will always be your strength,
Just open your eyes and you will find them.

The pain is not forever,
Every pain will end,
Be sure you did all you could,
To help to ease the pain
Before it's too late.

I am Always There

Knowing the end was close,
He dialled the number for home,
He knew the children would be climbing into bed,
His wife would be flustered,
His timing was all wrong,
But he knew it was the last chance to hear her say,
I love you.

When her voice came on the phone,
He smiled and breathed deeply,
He would give anything to hold her in his arms,
To kiss his children good night,
To read a bedtime story,
And then fight to get them to sleep before saying
I love you.

Recognising the pain in his voice,
She handed the phone to the children,
The tears filling her glossy eyes,
Fighting to stay strong as she listened to his voice,
'Daddy, when are you coming home?'
The tears broke free as she mimed,
I love you.

'I'm already there', was all he could say,
The children peered around,

'I am always there, I will never leave',
The children still could not see,
'I am watching you, playing with you',
She sobbed weakly and turned away,
'I love you'.

'Daddy, where are you?"
'I'm right beside you; I'm your imaginary friend'
The children smiled and nodded,
'Put mummy back on the phone'.
'Is there no chance?' she asked in a sob,
She hurried the children into bed,
'I love you'.

There was a silence on the phone,
Both knew the answer,
But neither one spoke it,
'I will always be with you, no matter what, no matter where',
She dropped to the floor,
Staring at her wedding ring,
'I love you'.

And then the phone cut off,
A sob broke free with a tear,
She knew the time had come,
She always knew it would,
But not like this, not on the phone,
She dropped the phone to her lap and said,

'I love you'.

And now she sits alone,
Rocking in her chair,
The children play outside,
Her parents watch over them like guardian angels,
Forever feeling alone,
She sobs and whispers,
'I love you'.

'Mummy, daddy say's hello',
A small voice comes from the door,
She lifts her eyes to see her youngest,
'Sweetie, daddy is in Heaven' she chokes on her words,
'No, daddy says hello',
She shakes her head and listens to her say,
'I love you'.

'Those were my last words to you',
She turns and stares again,
'What did you just say?'
'Daddy says I love you, and will always love you',
She shakes her head again and watches,
'What does Daddy say now?'
'I love you.'

'All those nights we spent together,
All those nights we spent apart,

Forever my love will live on,
Even well beyond the grave',
A smile slowly lights her face,
She slowly drops to her knees,
'I never got to tell you, I love you'.

A Precious Treasure

For nine months I wait to see you,
For nine months you wait to break free,
For nine months I hope and pray,
That all goes well from your head to toes, shoulders to knees.

I cannot wait to meet you,
You that I call my child,
My excitement grows day by day,
What will you be, quiet and calm or loud and wild?

Here you are my little one,
So delicate and small to measure,
How beautiful you are,
My precious little treasure.

You have grown so fast,
You're so strong and proud,
I once asked a question,
Now I know, wild and loud.

I am awake all day and now at night,
Darling, don't scream,
You're safe now, mummy's here,
It's just a bad dream.

Relax my little angel,

For nothing can hurt you now,
It doesn't matter how old you get,
Pain and fear I will never allow.

For you my darling child,
I will give you all my love,
I will never stop protecting you,
Even when I smile from up above.

Dark Changes

There was a time that I smiled,
And willingly dialled
Your number to hear your voice,
But now I consciously make the choice
To avoid your call,
Because I'm tired of the same heart breaking fall.

You are blind to the pain you cause,
You deserve a round of applause,
Congratulations, you're the first on my list,
In my life you're nothing more than a cyst,
You'll be the first to go,
And nothing about it will be slow.

For years I have stood by and hoped,
Heaven only knows how I coped,
You cast me out so oft,
But I was weak and soft,
I never dared to question your rejection,
But look at me now, strong without your affection.

At first, I hated the way I had changed,
But now I see it is good to be estranged
From you and your unwillingness to care,
We could have been such a pair,
But instead you ripped out my soul,

And now I have closed the hole.

You may never return to my life,
Never more will I walk on the edge of a knife,
From now I please only me,
I have broken free
From your tight hold,
And my heart has grown cold.

These changes make me strong,
And I realise now that I was wrong
To waste so much time,
Was practically a vicious crime,
Now I can smile once again,
For I have cast out the ever present pain.

Now the old me has died,
My useless tears have dried,
I stand with my head held high,
Wiser and never to be touched by the lie,
I have learned my lesson of love,
Love is weak and will fly like the dove.

The Ticking of the Clock

The snow settles,
The flowers grow,
The sun shines,
The leaves fall.

The child is born,
The child grows,
The child learns,
The child works.

You smile,
You cry,
You laugh,
You frown.

You love,
You hate,
You care,
You break.

The clock ticks on,
You grow old,
You regret the past,
And the things you never did.

Tick tock, tick tock,

You begin to think,
I should have done that,
I should have done this.

The angel smiles down on you,
The clock face twists,
Tock tick, tock tick,
Twelve to one.

You are young again,
Do it now,
You have the chance,
Will you change the world?

A tattoo,
A piercing,
Learning, laughing, loving,
And now you are back.

You have no regrets,
But what did you do?
You changed nothing,
The world is the same.

You are old,
You are dying,
But you are happy,
You have no regrets.

Moulding Minds

We teach our children a, b, c,
We teach our children 1, 2, 3,
We teach our children how to love,
We teach our children how to hate,
We teach our children how to share,
We teach our children how to care.

Every child is born the same,
You are the only one to take the blame,
Your child does not know how to love,
Your child does not know how to hate,
You showed them the way,
You led them astray.

A child does not know of their race,
There is no difference in their face,
A child does not understand love,
A child does not understand hate,
You told them that they were gay,
You taught them of foul play.

A child sees nothing wrong in life,
You gave words in the form of a knife,
You taught love,
You taught hate,
You corrupted their sweet mind,

With wicked words you made them blind.

A child does not know to say stop,
What would do you if your positions swap,
Will they show love?
Will they show hate?
What if it is your child?
That sweet name being filed.

But that will never be,
You will never have to plea,
Love is here,
Hate is here,
But they will not do the same to you,
Because they have experienced the hatred too.

Love Poem without the Letter 'e'
Inspired by a task during my studies.

For too long I saw your pain,
My aching soul holds you tight,
I know light took you from my arms,
But you are always with us.
My soul holds your autograph,
Profound and unforgiving,
And your charm marks my body.
In this world,
So many aim for our lost passion,
And now I cry for you,
Lost and fading into oblivion,
I cannot stop missing you.

So Many Names

So many names,
And yet you are invisible,
You do so much,
And yet you are taken for granted,
You are ever present,
And yet no one realises until you're gone.

You are called
Mum, mummy, mother, mama,
You are known around the world,
Mămică, mami, cici, ama,
You don't always fell appreciated,
But you are special and important.

We never say it,
But you are forever needed in our life,
We love to make you proud,
My true happiness comes from the smile you give,
Forever my protector,
Forever my mămică until the end of days.

My love,
Like yours, is eternal,
I will stand by you as you stand by me,
We will laugh through the years,
We may fight and cry,

But we will never part for a moment.

The distance between us has grown,
But I am still beside you,
Just close your eyes and you will see,
You will always come before all else,
Forever my strength,
You gave life and now I free you to live yours.

As we go our separate ways,
Do not fear for what we had,
It is still there,
Waiting for when we come together again,
The box protects us,
All will return to the way it was.

My Words Part Us

I know I must write this,
Though I know we will be kept apart,
My love for you grows,
Yet I have not met you,
You are my only love,
And still I cannot see you,
I know not what you look like,
Or where in the world you come from.
But I know you are the one,
I hope to Heaven you read this,
For these are the words I want you to hear,
But I know,
In your presence,
They will not come to me.
You are my sweet angel,
My beauty and my treasure,
Live your life to the full,
I cannot wait to hear of your stories,
I smile at the thought of your voice,
How you will sound is a mystery to me,
But know that no matter what,
My love will never drift or fade,
My loyalty will remain true,
My love strong,
My passion forever.
Our love will be eternal,

True until the end,
But I will not stop loving you.
We will grow old together,
And every day until the day I die,
I will tell you you're beautiful,
No one can compete,
You have my heart,
My eyes will never wander,
Forever my love for you.

My Eyes

I have been asked a few times what it is I see when I look at the world and I have been told to get my head out of the clouds. Here is my answer to what I see...

The earth is dull and grey,
The concrete world rages on,
The people rush by as I stand and watch,
Manners have all but disappeared,
I see smiles and tears mingle,
No one gives, they only take,
Everyone wants more,
No respect remains.

Forever destroying nature,
Building their towers taller than the last,
Fighting to be the best,
Demanding the spotlight,
Lies and cheats,
Forever spending what we do not have,
Pushing for power,
Lying for a non-existent love.

Lust over love,
Sacred acts destroyed,
Children being corrupted by once true role models,
Short dresses and no dignity,
Women returned to being a prize,

No longer a prize to show off,
But a prize to laugh at.

These girls destroy what we have fought for,
Their stupidity spreads like wild fire,
They do not see,
Beauty comes from within,
Not from the make-up and short dresses,
No man will love that, only lust for it,
He will take what he can,
But give nothing back.

You say my head is in the clouds,
You say I am off with the fairies,
But yet it is you living in this dream world,
I see the world for what it is,
You see it through rose tinted glasses,
Remove them now and change the world,
Life your life,
But do not regret your youth when you look back.

My Final Words

Live,
Love,
Smile,
Laugh,
Regret Nothing,
Live For Everything,
Die For Something.

**LEEDS LIBRARY AND
INFORMATION SERVICES**

821

21/7/2025

Printed in Dunstable, United Kingdom

63790374R10040